The Westing

L-I-T *Guiae*
Literature **In** Teaching

By Ellen Raskin

A Study Guide for Grades 5 and Up
Prepared by Charlotte S. Jaffe and Barbara T. Doherty
Illustrated by Koryn Agnello

ISBN 1-56644-021-1

© 1999 Educational Impressions, Inc., Hawthorne, NJ

EDUCATIONAL IMPRESSIONS, INC.
Hawthorne, NJ 07507

Printed in the United States of America.

This study guide is based on the book *The Westing Game:*
  Copyright 1978 by Ellen Raskin
  Published by arrangement with E. P. Dutton, Inc.

The Westing Game
Written by Ellen Raskin

STORY SUMMARY

"Turtle" Wexler, a bike-riding teenager, lives with her parents and older sister in a high-rise apartment building on the shores of Lake Michigan. Shortly after moving into the luxurious Sunset Towers, Turtle and fifteen other strange tenants become involved in solving a murder, hoping to become heir to a fabulous fortune. The sixteen are challenged by Mr. Westing to a game of wits. Through his will, he reveals vague clues to help (or confuse) the players. Each story character behaves suspiciously. At different times in the story, each of them looks like the guilty party. Who could it be? Whom can you trust? Eight teams are formed. Some of the partners work well together. Some of the pairings form alliances with other teams. At last, all of the clues are pieced together, and the mystery is solved.

Meet the Author

Ellen Raskin

Award-winning author and illustrator Ellen Raskin was described as an "inveterate puzzle maker, a trickster, a razzle-dazzle sleight-of-hand artist." This special talent is greatly apparent in Raskin's creative mystery novels as well as in the picture books that she wrote and illustrated for young children.

Raskin was born on March 13, 1928, in Milwaukee, Wisconsin, the setting for *The Westing Game*. She attended the University of Wisconsin from 1945 to 1949. Her first career was as a commercial illustrator and designer. Raskin married Dennis Flanagan, an editor, in 1960. Although successful as a graphic artist, Raskin decided to concentrate on writing and illustrating books for children. Her first effort, *Nothing Ever Happens On My Block*, was published in 1966. "I always write five times as much material as I have to and then cut and cut, and make everything readable. The most important thing for me is the first few words, that first line to catch the reader," the author revealed.

Raskin authored fifteen picture books and then turned her attention to longer novels. *Figgs & Phantoms*, published in 1947, was also illustrated by Raskin. It is a mystery story that features creative and unusually named characters. Raskin's Newbery Medal book, *The Westing Game*, again displays her special gift for creating puzzle-mystery stories and eccentric story characters. Critics found the book to be trickier than the ordinary mystery story.

Sadly, *The Westing Game* was to be Ellen Raskin's last book. She died on August 8, 1984, in New York. She had one daughter, Susan Metcalf.

Vocabulary

Chapters 1 and 2: *Sunset Towers* and *Ghosts or Worse*

Use the words in the box to complete the sentences below. You may need to use your dictionary.

asylum	authentic	brambles	breach	cuisine	elegant	exclusive
dim	gaping	glance	glisten	impatiently	luxurious	precious
scanned	spasms	sprawled	stubble	throbbing	warped	

1. Only the _____ of the corn stalks was left in the field.

2. Her arm was _____ with pain; she was sure it was broken.

3. The _____ light made it hard to read.

4. Carrie _____ the list for the correct address.

5. The club was very _____; only a select few were admitted.

6. The sunlight caused the dew to _____ on the leaves.

7. John knew with just a _____ that someone had been in the room before him.

8. Her photo albums and scrapbooks were _____ to her.

9. The children _____ waited for the party to begin.

10. After she fell, Lisa was _____ on the ice.

11. The woman had very refined taste; her gown was very _____.

12. The apartment was decorated in a very _____, expensive manner.

13. Her legs were scratched as she ran through the _____.

14. The paleontologist tested the fossils and found them to be _____.

15. Chinese _____ can vary from province to province; the taste is quite different.

Five of the vocabulary words from the first part of this activity were not used. Write an original sentence using each of those words.

1. _____

2. _____

3. _____

4. _____

5. _____

Comprehension and Discussion Questions
Chapters 1 and 2: *Sunset Towers and Ghosts or Worse*

Answer the following questions in complete sentence form. Give examples from the story to support your response where possible.

1. What is ironic about the name Sunset Towers? What facts did you learn about the people associated with it?

_____

_____

_____

_____

2. Why was it strange to see smoke coming from the Westing house?

_____

_____

_____

_____

3. Why was Doug careful to avoid touching Turtle's braid?

_____

_____

_____

_____

4. If you were Turtle, would you have agreed to stay in the Westing house for two dollars a minute?

_____

_____

_____

_____

_____

Vocabulary
Chapters 3 and 4:
Tenants In And Out and *The Corpse Found*

Match the vocabulary words on the left to the definitions on the right. Place the correct letter on each line.

_____	1. averted	A.	very thin and bony
_____	2. craned	B.	an artificial or deceptive front
_____	3. grappled	C.	damaged; defaced
_____	4. devoured	D.	winced, as from pain or surprise
_____	5. caution	E.	severely; unmercifully
_____	6. severe	F.	something inherited
_____	7. vigil	G.	stretched (the neck)
_____	8. putrid	H.	turned away; prevented
_____	9. gaunt	I.	summoned: signaled
_____	10. facade	J.	forethought to avoid danger
_____	11. marred	K.	rigid; reserved; stern
_____	12. harshly	L.	wrestled; struggled
_____	13. beckoned	M.	rotten; foul-smelling
_____	14. legacy	N.	watch
_____	15. flinched	O.	ate greedily

Use any three vocabulary words from the first part of this activity in original sentences.

1. _____

2. _____

3. _____

Comprehension and Discussion Questions
Chapters 3 and 4:
Tenants In and Out and *The Corpse Found*

Answer the following questions in complete sentence form. Give examples from the story to support your response where possible.

1. Contrast the way Mrs. Wexler treated Angela with the way she treated Turtle.

_____

_____

_____

_____

2. Why didn't Chris tell his brother Theo about "the limper" he had seen?

_____

_____

_____

_____

3. Why did Turtle hope to remain in the Westing house for 25 minutes? What caused her to leave after 12 minutes?

_____

_____

_____

_____

4. What surprising news was in the letters from E. J. Plum?

_____

_____

_____

_____

Vocabulary

Chapter 5 and 6: *Sixteen Heirs* and *The Westing Will*

Define the following words as they were used in the story. You may wish to use your dictionary for help.

1. **afflicted:** _____

2. **appalled:** _____

3. **audible:** _____

4. **dastardly:** _____

5. **elfin:** _____

6. **eccentric:** _____

7. **executor:** _____

8. **morbid:** _____

9. **purported:** _____

10. **relinquishing:** _____

11. **reproachful:** _____

12. **simpered:** _____

13. **sporadic:** _____

14. **trousseau:** _____

15. **verified:** _____

Choose three vocabulary words from the first part of this activity. Use those words to build word webs. Place one vocabulary word in each circle. Then fill in the blanks with words that are related to the center word. Stretch your imagination and try to think of some unusual connections. An example is given.

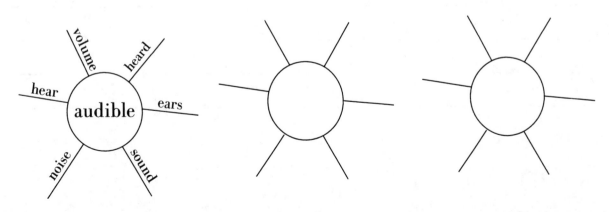

Comprehension and Discussion Questions
Chapter 5 and 6: *Sixteen Heirs* and *The Westing Will*

Answer the following questions in complete sentence form. Give examples from the story to support your response where possible.

1. Of what did Sydelle Pulaski's striped dress remind Turtle?

_____

_____

_____

_____

2. Do you think the potential heirs were really his nieces and nephews?

_____

_____

_____

_____

3. According to the will, who would inherit the windfall?

_____

_____

_____

_____

4. Judge the following comment made by Mr. Hoo: "The poor are crazy, the rich just eccentric."

_____

_____

_____

_____

Vocabulary

Chapters 7 and 8: *The Westing Game* and *The Paired Heirs*

PART I: For each set circle the word that is most **LIKE** the first one in meaning.

1. **buttressed:**   reinforced   weakened   unfortified

2. **hodgepodge:**   jumble   element   pure

3. **impeccable:**   flawed   flawless   imperfect

4. **incompetent:**   unqualified   effective   suitable

5. **inscrutable:**   understandable   knowing   puzzling

6. **instilled:**   implanted   withdrew   emptied

7. **vindictiveness:**   kindness   spitefulness   ruthlessness

PART TWO: For each set circle the word that is most **UNLIKE** the first one in meaning.

1. **divisive:**   unifying   shattering   unbroken

2. **greed:**   sharing   thrift   generosity

3. **pompous:**   rude   humble   conceited

4. **pretentious:**   ambitious   showy   modest

5. **refine:**   elevate   improve   taint

6. **relentless:**   unwilling   persistent   yielding

7. **repent:**   rejoice   apologize   amend

Comprehension and Discussion Questions

Chapters 7 and 8: *The Westing Game* and *The Paired Heirs*

Answer the following questions in complete sentence form. Give examples from the story to support your response where possible.

1. Why were Mrs. Wexler and Mr. Hoo upset that their spouses weren't at the meeting?

_____

_____

_____

_____

2. Why didn't Judge Ford believe that Westing had been murdered?

_____

_____

_____

_____

3. Judge the fact that Angela checked in Turtle's diary and took the newspaper from her desk drawer? Did her behavior surprise you?

_____

_____

_____

_____

4. Chart the clues that were given so far. Do you have any ideas about the message given in the clues?

_____

_____

_____

_____

Vocabulary

Chapters 9 and 10: *Lost And Found* and *The Long Party*

Complete each analogy by using a vocabulary word from the box. You may wish to use a dictionary. Some words will not be used.

coiffure	defiantly	embrace	exquisite	filigree	glumly
grimaced	hors d'oeuvre	informal	maiden	muffle	opted
paternal	sappy	scornful	timid	topaz	wheedled

1. happily is to joyfully as disobediently is to _____

2. wind is to gale as hug is to _____

3. unusual is to strange as casual is to _____

4. lift is to raise as deaden is to _____

5. cake is to dessert as shrimp cocktail is to _____

6. fabric is to lace as wire is to _____

7. flower is to lilac as jewel is to _____

8. jumped is to leaped as winced is to _____

9. automobile is to car as _____ is to hair style

10. recovered is to lost as complimentary is to _____

11. purified is to sanitized as chose is to _____

12. maternal is to mother as _____ is to father

13. outgoing is to friendly as _____ is to shy

14. severe is to harsh as sentimental is to _____

15. slowly is to quickly as _____ is to happily

Three words were not used. Use those words to create original analogies.

1. _____

2. _____

3. _____

Comprehension and Discussion Questions
Chapters 9 and 10: *Lost And Found* and *The Long Party*

Answer the following questions in complete sentence form. Give examples from the story to support your responses where possible.

1. What were the business papers referred to on the index card on the elevator wall?

_____

_____

_____

_____

2. Judge Mrs. Wexler's treatment of Turtle.

_____

_____

_____

_____

3. According to Mr. Hoo, how had he been wronged by Mr. Westing?

_____

_____

_____

4. Why did Judge Ford conclude that Mrs. Wexler was not related to Mr. Westing?

_____

_____

_____

_____

Vocabulary

Chapters 11 and 12: *The Meeting* and *The First Bomb*

Use the words in the box to complete the following sentences. You may need to use your dictionary.

> **alibis**   **implication**   **intended**   **larcenist**   **lured**   **panic**
>
> **paraphenalia**   **postpone**   **scoffed**   **sequined**   **shrieked**
>
> **speckled**   **swift**   **wispy**   **woozy**   **vault**

1. Both suspects had _____ for the time of the robbery.

2. The spilled paint _____ my books and desk.

3. Caught in a trap, the bird _____ loudly.

4. Everyone was in a state of _____ after the earthquake.

5. The _____ gown sparkled from afar.

6. My friends _____ at my idea and called it outrageous.

7. Bobby was so _____ that he was hard to catch.

8. The jewel thief was a _____.

9. The accident victim was so _____ that he could hardly speak.

10. George was able to _____ over every obstacle along the path.

11. Thin, _____ clouds were overhead.

12. Rain forced us to _____ the class picnic for one week.

13. A special food treat _____ our cat out of hiding.

14. Our camping equipment and _____ were soaked from the storm.

15. Jim didn't actually say so, but the _____ was that Bob was lying.

16. Liz didn't tell the others her plan until she learned what they _____ to do.

Comprehension and Discussion Questions
Chapters 11 and 12: *The Meeting* and *The First Bomb*

Answer the following questions in complete sentence form. Give examples from the story to support your response where possible.

1. How did Ms. Pulaski protect the information in the notes she took at the reading of the will?

_____

_____

_____

_____

2. Why, do you think, did Turtle lie to Mrs. Baumbach about her name? How did she get her nickname?

_____

_____

_____

_____

3. Do you think there was a bomb in the coffee shop? What does the chapter title tell us?

_____

_____

_____

4. Turtle said that Angela didn't really want to marry Denton. Find examples in this and previous chapters that might support this opinion.

_____

_____

_____

_____

Vocabulary

Chapters 13 and 14: *The Second Bomb* and *Pairs Repaired*

Each of the clues below is answered by one of the vocabulary words in the box. The letters in the squares will spell out a word which has something to do with the story. Not all of the words will be used.

---

accustomed   amends   awed   bestowed   bodice   debris   demeaning

distraught   fiancé   flask   hapless   lurking   mementoes   obsequious

petrified   protruding   ritual   superb   timidity   woefully

---

1. used to   _ _ [_] _ _ _ _ _ _ _

2. unfortunate   [_] _ _ _ _ _ _

3. submissive; fawning   _ _ _ [_] _ _ _ _ _

4. top, fitted part of dress   _ _ _ _ [_] _

5. lying in wait; sneaking   _ _ _ [_] _ _ _

6. souvenirs   _ _ [_] _ _ _ _ _

7. a ceremonial act   _ _ _ _ [_] _

8. presented as an honor; conferred   _ _ _ [_] _ _ _ _

9. very afraid; stunned with terror   _ [_] _ _ _ _ _ _ _

Use at least five unused vocabulary words to describe an event from Chapter 13 or Chapter 14. Underline the vocabulary words in your sentences. Draw a picture of the event.

_____

_____

_____

_____

_____

_____

Comprehension and Discussion Questions
Chapters 13 and 14: *The Second Bomb* and *Pairs Repaired*

Answer the following questions in complete sentence form. Give examples from the story to support your response where possible.

1. Do you think Mr. Hoo misjudged Doug? Why? Why not?

_____

_____

_____

_____

2. Of whom did Angela remind Flora Baumbach?

_____

_____

_____

_____

3. What made Chris feel that he and Sydelle had become real friends?

_____

_____

_____

_____

4. How did the authorities explain the two explosions? Why was it humorous that Jake wondered about the odds of having two explosions in two days in the same building?

_____

_____

_____

_____

Vocabulary
Chapter 15: *Fact and Gossip*

Alphabetize the words in the box. Then define them as they were used in the story.

guffaw cunning profound fateful scowl promote restraining

presided chemise venom soothsayer interrogate hack smirking

1. _____

2. _____

3. _____

4. _____

5. _____

6. _____

7. _____

8. _____

9. _____

10. _____

11. _____

12. _____

13. _____

14. _____

Create a word search of the vocabulary words. Exchange with a classmate to solve.

Comprehension and Discussion Questions
Chapter 15: *Fact and Gossip*

Answer the following questions in complete sentence form. Give examples from the story to support your response where possible.

1. Guess why Turtle listened to her transistor radio in school.

_____

_____

_____

_____

2. Why didn't Theo agree with Otis that there hadn't been a murder?

_____

_____

_____

_____

3. Do you think Dr. Wexler liked his wife working in the restaurant?

_____

_____

_____

_____

4. George Theodorakis didn't tell them about his connection with the Westings. Describe that connection. Evaluate his decision not to tell anyone.

_____

_____

_____

_____

Vocabulary

Chapters 16 and 17: *The Third Bomb* and *Some Solutions*

Use the words and phrases in the box to complete the sentences below. You may need to use your dictionary.

---

incriminated   suspicious   vehicular   painstakingly   erupted

jittery   reassured   impractical   trembled   despondently

vaguely   pranks   justice   kneel   scorched   culled   sneering   smirking

---

1. Lori _____ arranged the photos in her new album.

2. Because it was so foggy, Jordan could _____ see the outline of the mountains.

3. April Fool's Day is often the time for _____.

4. She accidentally _____ her blouse while she was ironing it.

5. My little brother is _____ of strangers.

6. The high cost of materials made the structure _____ to build.

7. Kim's family _____ her that she would soon feel fine again.

8. The bride and bridegroom seemed _____ before the wedding.

9. _____ traffic clogged the highway during the morning rush hour.

10. The steam _____ from the pot when the cover was removed.

11. The detective discovered evidence that _____ the suspect as the thief.

12. He had to _____ behind the couch to avoid being seen.

13. Our local judge's decisions are always made on the basis of _____.

14. The man reacted _____ to the bad news.

15. The children _____ with fear as they entered the creaking and vacant old house.

Three words weren't used in the first part of this activity. Use each of these words in an original sentence.

1. _____

2. _____

3. _____

Comprehension and Discussion Questions
Chapters 16 and 17: *The Third Bomb* and *Some Solutions*

Answer the following questions in complete sentence form. Give examples from the story to support your response where possible.

1. Explain Angela's thought, "Lucky Turtle, the neglected child."

_____

_____

_____

_____

2. Who was the bomber? What clues led us to the identity of the bomber? Why did she tilt the box toward herself, thereby causing injury to herself?

_____

_____

_____

_____

3. Give evidence to show how the heirs were becoming unnerved.

_____

_____

_____

_____

4. What surprising information linked James Hoo to Sam Westing?

_____

_____

_____

_____

Vocabulary
Chapters 18 and 19: *The Trackers* and *Odd Relatives*

Match the vocabulary words on the left to the definitions on the right. Place the correct letter on each line.

_____ 1. ailment   A. strong and muscular

_____ 2. apparent   B. hard, thickened place on skin

_____ 3. bachelor   C. held tightly

_____ 4. burly   D. continuous; prolonged

_____ 5. callus   E. to move around restlessly

_____ 6. chronic   F. foot doctor

_____ 7. clasped   G. skillful handling

_____ 8. distorted   H. payment paid to obtain a captive's release

_____ 9. fidget   I. ran hurriedly

_____ 10. hostage   J. easy to see; obvious

_____ 11. manipulation   K. wandering from place to place without a means of livelihood

_____ 12. podiatrist   L. changed; misshapen

_____ 13. ransom   M. act of punishment in return for a wrong

_____ 14. scampered   N. a mild illness

_____ 15. vagrancy   O. person held as a pledge that certain terms will be met

_____ 16. vengeance   P. unmarried man

Create a Character
If you could add another character to the list of would-be heirs to the Westing fortune, who might it be? Create a new character and use some of the vocabulary words in this unit in your description.

_____

_____

_____

_____

_____

Comprehension and Discussion Questions
Chapters 18 and 19: *The Trackers* and *Odd Relatives*

Answer the following questions in complete sentence form. Give examples from the story to support your response where possible.

1. Why did Turtle crumple the newspaper when Flora spoke lovingly about Rosalie?

_____

_____

_____

_____

2. Chris's third visitor of the day brought hopeful news. Describe the news and Chris's reaction to it.

_____

_____

_____

_____

3. How did Turtle show creativity in keeping up with the stock market report?

_____

_____

_____

_____

4. Explain Sam Westing's big mistake.

_____

_____

_____

_____

Vocabulary

Chapters 20 and 21: *Confessions* and *The Fourth Bomb*

Define the following words according to their use in the story.

1. **advantage:** _____

2. **arsenal:** _____

3. **attorney:** _____

4. **blabbering:** _____

5. **blackmail:** _____

6. **composure:** _____

7. **decaying:** _____

8. **delinquent:** _____

9. **distracted:** _____

10. **embarrass:** _____

11. **fuming:** _____

12. **grimy:** _____

13. **immigrate:** _____

14. **interrogation:** _____

15. **legitimate:** _____

16. **loathe:** _____

17. **miscalculation:** _____

18. **remedy:** _____

Word Categories

After you have defined the words, place them into as many different categories, or groups, as possible. Give each category a title. You may use the same word in more than one category. At least two words are needed to comprise a category. Compare results among your classmates. Some examples follow:

<table>
<tr><td>FOUND IN COURTROOM</td><td>VERBS</td></tr>
<tr><td>attorney   delinquent</td><td>blabbering   embarrass</td></tr>
</table>

Comprehension and Discussion Questions
Chapters 20 and 21: *Confessions* and *The Fourth Bomb*

Answer the following questions in complete sentence form. Give examples from the story to support your response where possible.

1. Explain why Theo was suspected of being the bomber?

_____

_____

_____

_____

2. According to the judge, which heir did Sam Westing want punished? Explain.

_____

_____

_____

_____

3. Why did Turtle agree to allow Theo to use her bike? What would you have done if you had been Turtle?

_____

_____

_____

_____

4. What did Sydelle and Angela conclude about the clues?

_____

_____

_____

_____

Vocabulary
Chapters 22 and 23: *Losers, Winners* and *Strange Answers*

PART I: For each set circle the word that is most **LIKE** the first one in meaning.

1. **anxious:**   apologetic   worried   happy

2. **capital:**   debt   power   money

3. **derisive:**   mocking   cheating   angry

4. **exquisite:**   pure   beautiful   expensive

5. **flask:**   bottle   dish   utensil

6. **mimicked:**   flattered   imitated   frightened

7. **pompous:**   proud   popular   pleasing

PART TWO: For each set circle the word that is most **UNLIKE** the first one in meaning.

1. **dejected**   pretty   smart   happy

2. **despair:**   sorrow   jealousy   optimism

3. **distracted**   focused   diverted   distorted

4. **reluctant**   resistant   willing   hesitant

5. **slurred**   messy   distinct   neat

6. **somber**   cheerful   gloomy   scared

7. **spacious**   wide   thick   cramped

Comprehension and Discussion Questions
Chapters 22 and 23: *Losers, Winners* and *Strange Answers*

Answer the following questions in complete sentence form. Give examples from the story to support your response where possible.

1. Who was the burglar? How do we know?

_____

_____

_____

_____

2. Explain Grace's remark, "Look, there she is, the mother of Cain and Abel."

_____

_____

_____

_____

3. Why did Judge Ford believe that Sam Westing might still be alive? Who, did she think, was in danger from him?

_____

_____

_____

_____

4. Theo responded, "No answer." Why?

_____

_____

_____

_____

Vocabulary
Chapters 24 and 25: *Wrong All Wrong* and *Westing's Wake*

For each sentence, circle the most appropriate definition for the word in bold type as it is used in the sentence. Use your dictionary to help you.

1. The criminal was quickly **apprehended** by the police.

    arrested   questioned   followed

2. That **cunning** boy outwitted his enemies.

    quick   strong   clever

3. An unexpected toothache filled me with **agony**.

    surprise   pain   anger

4. The **culprit** who broke the window should pay to fix it.

    victim   accuser   offender

5. Samantha was **fanatical** about keeping her room neat.

    zealous   lazy   careless

6. The boy's angry **glare** showed his disapproval.

    voice   stare   gesture

7. My little sister **impatiently** awaited her turn to play the game.

    politely   calmly   restlessly

8. Dr. Deere thought the heirs were suffering from **paranoia**.

    stomach sickness   mental disorder   memory loss

9. The long climb up the steep steps caused his heart to **throb**.

    beat fast   hurt   slow down

10. The **mischievous** students played a prank on their classmate.

    naughty   unhappy   silly

Comprehension and Discussion Questions
Chapters 24 and 25: *Wrong All Wrong* and *Westing's Wake*

Answer the following questions in complete sentence form. Give examples from the story to support your response where possible.

1. The document reminded them that "it is not what you have, it's what you don't have that counts." How did Sydelle use this clue to try to figure out the answer?

_____

_____

_____

_____

2. Why was the judge so sure that Sandy was really Sam Westing?

_____

_____

_____

_____

3. Mr. Westing said the ashes of his body would be scattered to the four winds. What are the four winds? Does this give you any ideas?

_____

_____

_____

_____

4. Turtle remembered that Sandy had bought a candle for his wife's birthday. Why is that important?

_____

_____

_____

_____

Vocabulary

Chapter 26: *Turtle's Trial*

Read each clue and find the answers in the box. Then use the letters above the numbered spaces to decipher the secret message. Some of the words will not be used.

---

baffled   furious   oath   imply   accomplice   aviator
duplicate   gesture   diagnosis   flaw   paused
benefactor   recipient   tenants   mull

---

1. an act made as a sign of intent
 __ __(6.) __ __(1.) __ __(19.) __

2. pilot
 __(9.) __ __ __ __(4.) __ __(3.)

3. puzzled
 __ __ __ __ __(5.) __(8.) __

4. error
 __ __(7.) __ __

5. angry
 __ __ __(10.) __ __ __ __(12.)

6. giver of financial or other aid
 __ __ __(11.) __(15.) __ __ __ __(13.) __ __

7. a promise
 __ __ __ __(14.)

8. waited
 __ __ __ __(16.) __(17.) __

9. partner
 __ __(18.) __ __ __ __ __ __ __(20.)

10. copied from an original
 __ __(2.) __ __ __ __ __ __(21.) __

The Secret Message

1	2	3	4	5	6		7	8	9	10	11	12
__	__	__	__	__	__		__	__	__	__	__	__

	13	14	15		16	17	18	19	20	21
	__	__	__		__	__	__	__	__	__

Comprehension and Discussion Questions
Chapter 26: *Turtle's Trial*

Answer the following questions in complete sentence form. Give examples from the story to support your response where possible.

1. Why did Turtle say to Otis Amber, "Mr. Amber, it seems that we are not all who we say we are"?

_____

_____

_____

_____

2. Evaluate the information that Turtle extracted from Denton Deere. Explain its importance.

_____

_____

_____

_____

3. What made Turtle sure that Sam Westing was Sandy the doorman?

_____

_____

_____

_____

4. The judge and Turtle both knew that Windy Windkloppel took three names. From what you have read so far, try to guess the identity of the fourth.

_____

_____

_____

_____

Vocabulary

Chapters 27 and 28: *A Happy Fourth* and *And Then...*

Define the following words according to their use in the story.

1. **arrogance:** _____

2. **bequeath:** _____

3. **consultant:** _____

4. **coroner:** _____

5. **discard:** _____

6. **discontented:** _____

7. **endorsed:** _____

8. **extravaganza:** _____

9. **inquiry:** _____

10. **panic:** _____

11. **resignation:** _____

12. **regrettable:** _____

13. **smoldering:** _____

14. **taut:** _____

Alliteration Creations

Alliteration is a literary device that is used by authors for a special effect. It is the repetition of the initial or beginning sounds in two or more words in a sentence.

Example: I **b**equeath to my **b**rother **B**ill my **b**est **b**ook.

Use words from the first part of this activity to create your own alliteration sentences. Share with your classmates.

_____

_____

_____

_____

_____

Comprehension and Discussion Questions
Chapters 27 and 28: *A Happy Fourth* and *And Then...*

Answer the following questions in complete sentence form. Give examples from the story to support your response where possible.

1. Why was Crow declared innocent?

_____

_____

_____

_____

2. How did Turtle figure out the fourth identity of Windy Windkloppel? Why did she call this person Sandy?

_____

_____

_____

_____

3. Explain how the judge finally repaid the favor that Sam Westing had done for her.

_____

_____

_____

_____

4. How had life changed for the Wexler family now that the "Westing Game" was over?

_____

_____

_____

_____

Vocabulary

Chapters 29 and 30: *Five Years Pass* and *The End?*

Match the vocabulary words on the left to the definitions on the right. Place the correct letter on each line.

_____	1. administration	A. person who gives legal advice
_____	2. appetizer	B. easily broken
_____	3. corporate	C. work involved in publishing a newspaper or a magazine
_____	4. correspondent	D. treatment of disorders of the skeletal system
_____	5. counsel	E. bright; glowing
_____	6. donation	F. pertaining to a corporation
_____	7. fiancé	G. expert in the study of the nervous system
_____	8. fragile	H. person who communicates by means of letters
_____	9. journalism	I. a gift or contribution
_____	10. legal	J. Latin-American dance
_____	11. neurologist	K. the management of an institution
_____	12. orthopedics	L. short, rough growth of beard
_____	13. qualified	M. man engaged to be married
_____	14. radiant	N. food served before a meal
_____	15. stubble	O. relating to or concerning the law
_____	16. tango	P. competent

Guess the Character

Use vocabulary words to describe some story characters. Then challenge your classmates to guess the mystery characters.

Example: Who is the **fiancé** of Sydelle Pulaski?

_____

_____

_____

_____

Comprehension and Discussion Questions
Chapters 29 and 30: *Five Years Pass* and *The End?*

Answer the following questions in complete sentence form. Give examples from the story to support your response where possible.

1. Why was Mr. Hoo no longer an angry person?

_____

_____

_____

_____

2. Explain T. R. Wexler's radiance. Whom did she defeat?

_____

_____

_____

_____

3. What surprising news did Turtle relate to Mr. Eastman about Angela? What surprising news did Mr. Eastman relate to Turtle about Angela?

_____

_____

_____

_____

4. Discuss the outcome of the story. Which parts seemed predictable? Unpredictable? What portion of the outcome would you change? Explain.

_____

_____

_____

_____

Spotlight Literary Skill
Plot

PART I:

A plot is a sequence of events that tells a story. You have just read *The Westing Game*. Put the following story events in the order as they occurred in the plot. Number the events from 1 through 15 with 1 being the first event to occur and 15 being the last.

_____ Judge Ford has a party.

_____ The partners get checks for $10,000.

_____ Sydelle's shorthand notebook is stolen.

_____ Turtle teaches Alice to play chess.

_____ Doug wins the mile-run as a high-school senior.

_____ Turtle sees a "corpse" in the Westing house.

_____ Angela is hospitalized.

_____ Sydelle fractures her ankle.

_____ Turtle and Flora make a big profit on the stock market when they sell their Westing stock.

_____ Sandy, the doorman, is declared dead by Doctor Sikes.

_____ A blizzard keeps everyone in Sunset Towers snowbound.

_____ Turtle visits Mr. Eastman and wins the "Westing Game."

_____ Angela marries Dr. Deere.

_____ Turtle makes a bet with Theo and Doug to stay in the Westing house for two dollars per minute.

_____ Judge Ford hires a private detective.

PART II:

Write three more story events below and have a classmate insert them in the proper place.

1. _____

2. _____

3. _____

Cooperative-Learning Activity
Create a Mystery

Try your hand at creating your own mystery story! Your class should be divided into small cooperative-learning groups in order to play this game.

1. Each group must create or gather four clues.
Example: candle, calendar (with a date circled), key, postcard.

2. Each set of clues is then placed in a **Mystery Envelope** with the group number written on it.

3. The numbered envelopes are exchanged among the groups. (No group keeps its own envelope.)

4. Each cooperative group must use the clues in the envelope to create an original mystery story. These clues must help to solve the mystery.

5. Remember to have interesting characters, settings, and a well-written plot. Be sure to include a motive for the crime!

6. The completed mystery stories can be presented to the whole class to solve.

Spotlight Literary Skill
Stereotyping

A **stereotype** is a character with exaggerated personality traits who falsely represents a group of people. Ellen Raskin stereotyped many of her characters to make them stand out in the reader's mind.

Read the list of characters below. Next to each name write one or more personality traits that make the character seem stereotyped.

Grace Wexler _____

_____

_____

Madame Hoo _____

_____

_____

Doug Hoo _____

_____

_____

Turtle Wexler _____

_____

_____

Dr. Denton Deere _____

_____

_____

Sydelle Pulaski _____

_____

_____

Critic's Corner

Pretend that you are writing a review of *The Westing Game* for your daily newspaper. Your job is to provide information about the book and to evaluate it for your readers. Be sure to include the setting, plot, and characterization as well as your general opinion. Among the things to consider are the believability of the plot and characters, the appropriateness of the vocabulary, and the writing style of the author. Fill in the outline to help you organize your ideas. Then write your review on another paper.

TITLE: *The Westing Game*

AUTHOR: Ellen Raskin

SETTING: _____

_____

_____

_____

_____

DESCRIPTION OF THE MAIN CHARACTERS: _____

_____

_____

_____

_____

SUMMARY OF THE PLOT: _____

_____

_____

_____

_____

GENERAL OPINION OF THE STORY: _____

_____

_____

_____

_____

More Post-Reading Activities
The Westing Game

1. Create a board game based on *The Westing Game*. Include major events and characters from the story. Create a booklet to accompany the game; include the game's object and rules.

2. "Nothing is what is seems to be" was a clue that was given to the heirs. Present some optical illusions to your classmates to prove that saying is true.

3. Choose one of the story characters and create a diary of story events as told from that character's point of view.

4. In *The Westing Game*, many of the characters change dramatically during the course of the story. Make a chart that illustrates these changes for the following characters: Angela, Grace, Chris, Mr. Hoo, Turtle, and Jake.

5. Learn to play chess. This tricky game of strategy is an important influence on the plot of *The Westing Game*.

6. With other members of your cooperative-learning group, write a script based on the novel. Present your finished product to classmates and parents.

7. Throughout the novel, Ellen Raskin used humor to help her weave her mystery. Find three examples of humor and tell how its use adds to the story.

8. *The Westing Game* was the winner of the prestigious Newbery Award. Tell why, in your opinion, this book did or did not deserve the honor.

9. Dialogue, the spoken words of the characters, is an important feature of most types of writing. Through dialogue, we learn more about how each character thinks, feels, and relates to others. With your cooperative-learning group, create an imaginary dialogue that might have taken place among several characters in the story. Present your dialogue in the form of a skit to the entire class.

Crossword Puzzle
The Westing Game

See how much you remember about *The Westing Game*. Have fun!

ACROSS

1. T. R. Wexler made millions here.
5. A dressmaker.
8. State in which story is set.
10. Turtle's father.
12. Chris's hobby.
17. He married 4 Down.
18. Sam Westing's wife.
19. What a podiatrist treats.
20. Game enjoyed by Sam Westing and Turtle.
22. A bookie.
23. Engaged to Angela.
25. The doorman.
26. Her inclusion was a mistake.
28. Turtle's last name.
30. President and Chief Executive Officer of Westing Paper Products Corporation.
32. Sunset Towers was located on the shores of this lake.

DOWN

2. Where Mrs. Hoo wanted to go.
3. Author of *The Westing Game*.
4. Turtle's real name.
6. The delivery "boy."
7. Angela was one.
9. Turtle kicked people here if they touched her braid.
11. He pronounced Sandy dead.
12. November fifteenth was Crow's _____.
13. She falsely confessed to being the bomber.
14. An inventor.
15. Mother of Angela and Turtle.
16. Language in which 26 Across wrote her shorthand.
21. Nickname taken by Mrs. Hoo.
22. What J. J. Ford was.
24. First name of 3 Down.
27. Reason Turtle first entered the Westing house.
29. What Doug liked to do.
31. Postal abbreviation for 8 Across.

Glossary of Literary Terms

Alliteration: Repetition of initial (beginning) sounds in 2 or more consecutive or neighboring words.

Analogy: A comparison based upon the resemblance in some particular ways between things that are otherwise unlike.

Anecdote: A short account of an interesting, amusing, or biographical occurrence.

Anticlimax: An event that is less important than what occurred before it.

Archaic language: Language that was once common in a particular historic period but which is no longer commonly used.

Cause and effect: The relationship in which one condition brings about another condition as a direct result. The result, or consequence, is called the effect.

Character development: The ways in which the author shows how a character changes as the story proceeds.

Characterization: The method used by the author to give readers information about a character; a description or representation of a person's qualities or peculiarities.

Classify: To arrange according to a category or trait.

Climax: The moment when the action in a story reaches its greatest conflict.

Compare and contrast: To examine the likenesses and differences of two people, ideas, or things. (*Contrast* emphasizes differences. *Compare* may focus on likenesses alone or on likenesses and differences.)

Conflict: The main source of drama and tension in a literary work; the discord between persons or forces that brings about dramatic action.

Connotation: Something suggested or implied, not actually stated.

Description: An account that gives the reader a mental image or picture of something.

Dialect: A form of language used in a certain geographic region; it is distinguished from the standard form of the language by pronunciation, grammar, and/or vocabulary.

Dialogue (dialog): The parts of a literary work that represent conversation.

Fact: A piece of information that can be proven or verified.

Figurative language: Description of one thing in terms usually used for something else. Simile and metaphor are examples of figurative language.

Flashback: The insertion of an earlier event into the normal chronological sequence of a narrative.

Foreshadowing: The use of clues to give readers a hint of events that will occur later on.

Historical fiction: Fiction represented in a setting true to the history of the time in which the story takes place.

Imagery: Language that appeals to the senses; the use of figures of speech or vivid descriptions to produce mental images.

Irony: The use of words to express the opposite of their literal meaning.

Legend: A story handed down from earlier times; its truth is popularly accepted but can't be verified.

Limerick: Humorous 5-lined poem with form *aabba*. Lines 1, 2 and 5 are longer than lines 3 and 4.

Metaphor: A figure of speech that compares two unlike things without the use of "like" or "as."

Mood: The feeling that the author creates for the reader.

Motivation: The reasons for the behavior of a character.

Narrative: The type of writing that tells a story.

Narrator: The character who tells the story.

Opinion: A personal point of view or belief.

Parody: Writing that ridicules or imitates something more serious.

Personification: Figure of speech in which an inanimate object or an abstract idea is given human characteristics.

Play: A literary work written in dialogue form and usually performed before an audience.

Plot: The arrangement or sequence of events in a story.

Point of view: The perspective from which a story is told.

Protagonist: The main character.

Pun: A play on words that are similar in sound but different in meaning.

Realistic fiction: True-to-life fiction; people, places, and happenings are similar to those in real life.

Resolution: Part of the plot (from climax on) where the main dramatic conflict is worked out.

Satire: A literary work that pokes fun at individual or societal weaknesses.

Sequencing: The placement of story elements in the order of their occurrence.

Setting: The time and place in which the story occurs.

Simile: A figure of speech that uses "like" or "as" to compare two unlike things.

Stereotype: A character whose personality traits represent a group rather than an individual.

Suspense: Quality that causes readers to wonder what will happen next.

Symbolism: The use of a thing, character, object, or idea to represent something else.

Synonyms: Words that are very similar in meaning.

Tall tale: An exaggerated story detailing unbelievable events.

Theme: The main idea of a literary work; the message the author wants to communicate, sometimes expressed as a generalization about life.

Tone: The quality or feeling conveyed by the work; the author's style or manner of expression.

ANSWERS

Chapters 1 & 2: Vocabulary

1. stubble	4. scanned	7. glance	10. sprawled	13. brambles
2. throbbing	5. exclusive	8. precious	11. elegant	14. authentic
3. dim	6. glisten	9. impatiently	12. luxurious	15. cuisine

Chapters 1 & 2: Comprehension and Discussion Questions

1. Although the sun sets in the west, Sunset Towers faced east. Also, there were no towers. Among the tenants were a bookie, a burglar, and a bomber. The tenants were specially chosen; one was selected by mistake. The delivery "boy" who delivered the rental advertisements was sixty-two; he seemed to know a lot about the potential tenants.
2. No one had seen Westing in years. It was rumored that he was dead.
3. She kicked anyone who touched her braid in the shins. Doug was a runner and didn't want to chance injury to his legs.
4. Answers will vary, but Otis Amber's description of the corpse was rather scary!

Chapters 3 & 4: Vocabulary

1. H	4. O	7. N	10. B	13. I
2. G	5. J	8. M	11. C	14. F
3. L	6. K	9. A	12. E	15. D

Chapters 3 & 4: Comprehension and Discussion Questions

1. She seemed to favor Angela over Turtle. In Chapter 1 she said the small bedroom would be fine for Turtle. In Chapter 3 she commented that Angela had very delicate skin. She greeted Turtle with "Oh, it's you." She criticized Turtle's costume and said the dressmaker was too busy with Angela's gown to hem it.
2. He didn't want to spoil Theo's story.
3. She hoped to win enough to pay for a subscription to the *Wall Street Journal*. She found Sam Westing's corpse; however, it was not rotting. He was recently deceased.
4. Otis Amber and the others were named as beneficiaries in Westing's will.

Chapters 5 & 6: Comprehension and Discussion Questions

1. It reminded her of purple waves of grain. Otis had said that one of the kids who had entered the Westing house a year ago ran out saying "purple waves" over and over again.
2. Answers will vary, but it is unlikely.
3. Mr. Westing said that his life had been taken by one of the sixteen heirs. The heir who solved the mystery would inherit the windfall.
4. Answers will vary.

Chapters 7 & 8: Vocabulary

Part I

1. reinforced	3. flawless	5. puzzling	7. spitefulness
2. jumble	4. unqualified	6. implanted	

Part II

1. unifying	3. humble	5. taint	7. rejoice
2. generosity	4. modest	6. yielding	

Chapters 7 & 8: Comprehension and Discussion Questions

1. Mrs. Hoo and Mr. Wexler would not receive the $10,000 to share. They were out of the game.
2. Westing was so powerful that he would have insisted on police protection.
3. Answers may vary.
4. Chris and Dr. Deere: FOR/PLAIN/GRAIN/SHED
   Turtle and Flora: SEA/MT/AM/O
   Grace and Mr. Hoo: FRUITED/PURPLE/WAVES/FOR/SEA
   Doug and Theo: HIS/N/ON(NO)/TO/THEE/FOR
   Sandy and Judge Ford: SKIES/AM/SHINING/BROTHER
   Angela and Sydelle: GOOD/GRACE/FROM/HOOD/SPACIOUS
   Berthe Crow and Otis: not given
   NOTE: Some will probably realize that they are words from "America the Beautiful."

Chapters 9 & 10: Vocabulary

1. defiantly	4. muffle	7. topaz	10. scornful	13. timid
2. embrace	5. hors' d'oeuvre	8. grimaced	11. opted	14. sappy
3. informal	6. filigree	9. coiffure	12. paternal	15. glumly

Chapters 9 & 10: Comprehension and Discussion Questions

1. Someone had stolen Sydelle Pulaski's shorthand version of Westing's will.
2. Answers will vary, but the only time she spoke nicely to Turtle was when she tried to get Turtle to show her her clues. She was very insensitive to Turtle's feelings: ". . . everything I own goes to Angela."
3. Mr. Westing had stolen his idea for disposable diapers.
4. Mrs. Wexler said that he was related on her father's side. If the relationship she described had been true, her maiden name would have been Westing.

Chapters 11 & 12: Vocabulary

1. alibis	5. sequined	9. woozy	13. lured
2. speckled	6. scoffed	10. vault	14. paraphenalia
3. shrieked	7. swift	11. wispy	15. implication
4. panic	8. larcenist	12. postpone	16. intended

Chapters 11 & 12: Comprehension and Discussion Questions

1. She wrote the shorthand notes in Polish. She didn't think the idea of equal shares was fair because she had been the only one to think of taking notes.
2. Answers may vary. Perhaps she didn't like her name. She got her nickname because her mother thought that as a baby she looked like a turtle when she stuck her head out of her blanket.
3. Answers will vary. The chapter title tells us there will be at least one more bomb.
4. Angela hurried out of the room when Denton whispered his diagnosis of Chris's condition. (Chapter 5) She didn't have on her engagement ring because of a rash on her finger. (Chapter 9) She wondered why everyone asked about Denton all the time. It annoyed her that people acted as if she was nobody without him. (Chapter 10) When her mother discussed the catering of her wedding shower, Angela ran into Judge Ford's kitchen. (Chapter 10) She left her ring on the sink. (Chapter 12)

Chapters 13 & 14: Vocabulary

1. accustomed	4. bodice	7. ritual
2. hapless	5. lurking	8. bestowed
3. obsequious	6. mementoes	9. petrified

The word spelled out is "checkmate."

Chapters 13 & 14: Comprehension and Discussion Questions

1. He called him lazy because he hadn't come to the restaurant early; however, no one had told him that it would be opening early because of the damage to the coffee shop.
2. She reminded her of Violet Westing, Sam Westing's daughter who had drowned.
3. Sydelle wasn't afraid to ask him pointed questions about his physical condition.
4. They said they were natural gas explosions. It was humorous that Jake wondered about the odds because we just found out he was a bookie.

Chapter 15: Comprehension and Discussion Questions

1. She was probably listening to the stock report.
2. If there had been no murder, he thought, there could be no answer and no winner.
3. Answers may vary, but he seemed slightly annoyed that she didn't pay more attention to him: "Hello to you, too.") He asked, "What's new with you," implying that he hadn't seen much of her.
4. Rumor was that Sam Westing's daughter had wanted to marry him. She killed herself rather than marry the man she was expected to marry.

Chapters 16 & 17: Vocabulary

1. painstakingly	4. scorched	7. reassured	10. erupted	13. justice
2. vaguely	5. suspicious	8. jittery	11. incriminated	14. despondently
3. pranks	6. impractical	9. vehicular	12. kneel	15. trembled

Chapters 16 & 17: Comprehension and Discussion Questions

1. Angela envied Turtle because Grace Wexler did not have the same high expectations for Turtle. Turtle had more freedom to do what she wanted to do.
2. Angela was the bomber. Clues: She looked at her watch; her hands were shaking; she unknotted the gold ribbon slowly; and she pushed Turtle away as the lid blasted off. She tilted the box toward herself so that Turtle

wouldn't get hurt.

3. The heirs called the bomb squad several times to examine packages. Grace made her husband eat the first piece of candy. When Turtle shouted, "Mrs. Baumbach," someone thought she had said, "bomb."

4. Hoo had sued Westing over the invention of the disposable paper diaper. He got $25,000 in a settlement and thought he was cheated.

Chapters 18 & 19: Vocabulary

1. N	5. B	9. E	13. H
2. J	6. D	10. O	14. I
3. P	7. C	11. G	15. K
4. A	8. L	12. F	16. M

Chapters 18 & 19: Comprehension and Discussion Questions

1. Turtle was jealous of Gloria's love for her daughter. She liked the attention she was getting from Flora. She did not get much from her own mother.

2. Dr. Deere told Chris of a hopeful new treatment. He offered to take Chris into the hospital to begin tests. At first Chris resented more hospitalization. Then he pretended that he was being taken against his will and began to enjoy the experience.

3. When Turtle got caught with a radio in her ear, she claimed she had a toothache and needed to listen to music. Then she kept asking permission to go to the lavatory, claiming she had a bladder infection.

4. Sam chose Sydelle Pulaski instead of Sybil Pulaski.

Chapters 20 & 21: Comprehension and Discussion Questions

1. Theo had been experimenting with chemical fertilizers. It was thought that he resented his parents working him too hard in the coffee shop.

2. Sam Westing wanted to punish the one who had hurt him the most. The judge believed he wanted his former wife punished because he held her responsible for his daughter's suicide. She believed that one of the heirs was the former Mrs. Westing.

3. Theo threatened Turtle that he would tell the truth about Angela.

4. They reshuffled their collected clues and added one given by Dr. Deere and Chris. The result was the song "America, The Beautiful."

Chapters 22 & 23: Vocabulary

Part I

1. worried	3. mocking	5. bottle	7. proud
2. money	4. beautiful	6. imitated	

Part II

1. happy	3. focused	5. distinct	7. cramped
2. optimism	4. willing	6. cheerful	

Chapters 22 & 23: Comprehension and Discussion Questions

1. Mrs. Hoo was the burglar. She had Turtle's clock. In Chapter 9 Turtle had put up a note in the elevator in which she asked the thief to give it back.

2. In the Bible, Cain and Abel were brothers. Cain murdered Abel. Grace thought Turtle was the bomber who almost killed Angela. She felt people would be looking and sneering at her.

3. Turtle had said that the corpse looked like a wax figure. An old accident report said that Westing had suffered severe facial injuries. He could have had plastic surgery. She thought the former Mrs. Westing was in danger.

4. Theo changed his mind about accusing Otis Amber because he had seen him in the soup kitchen helping needy men.

Chapters 24 & 25: Vocabulary

1. arrested	3. pain	5. zealous	7. restlessly	9. beat fast
2. clever	4. offender	6. stare	8. mental disorder	10. naughty

Chapters 24 & 25: Comprehension and Discussion Questions

1. When arranged in order, the following letter groups were missing: BER, THE, ERICA, AND CROW.

2. In the chess game with Theo, Sandy had used the queen's sacrifice, a famous Westing trap. The judge had lost games to Westing this way. Westing had sacrificed his real queen, Crow.

3. The four winds are the currents blowing from each of the four cardinal points of the compass: north, south, east, and west. Some readers might realize that three of these have been used: Sam WESTing, Barney NORTHrup, and Sandy McSOUTHers. They might also realize that EAST is what's missing.

4. His wife was Crow, and it was Crow's birthday. Because it was a three-hour candle, she surmised that the game was still on and that they still had three hours to find the heir.

Chapter 26: Vocabulary

Part I

1. gesture	3. baffled	5. furious	7. oath	9. accomplice
2. aviator	4. flaw	6. benefactor	8. paused	10. duplicate

Part II

Turtle learns the secret.

Chapter 26: Comprehension and Discussion Questions

1. Otis was disguised as a delivery man, but was really a private investigator. She was quoting from the document.
2. Turtle hadn't kicked Sandy, but she had kicked Barney Northrup; therefore, she knew that Barney Northrup and Sandy McSouthers were the same person.
3. He had always used clever disguises in Fourth of July pageants. Neither character drank. Sam Westing as Sandy wrote the last part of the will.
4. Some might guess that Julian R. Eastman, President and Chief Executive Officer of the Westing Paper Products Corporation, was the fourth. East was the only "wind" not yet known to have been used as an alias by Windy Windkloppel. (He was first mentioned in Chapter 4.)

Chapters 27 & 28: Comprehension and Discussion Questions

1. The coroner determined that Sam Westing, alias Sandy McSouthers had died as a result of a heart attack. The coroner was part of the plot. (Sam Westing was not really dead.)
2. Turtle used the directions—west, north, and south—in the names of the identities. The fourth had "east" in it. Sandy and Windkoppel were the same person. She felt closest to him as Sandy, whom she considered her friend.
3. The judge used her share of Sunset Towers to pay for Chris's college education.
4. Jake was no longer a bookie nor a podiatrist. He became a state lottery consultant. Grace bought Hoo's On First and ran it very successfully. Angela was in medical school. Turtle was respected by her mother.

Chapters 29 & 30: Vocabulary

1. K	5. A	9. C	13. P
2. N	6. I	10. O	14. E
3. F	7. M	11. G	15. L
4. H	8. B	12. D	16. J

Chapters 29 & 30: Comprehension and Discussion Questions

1. Mr. Hoo was now successful. His Little Foot-Eze was sold in several cities. Doug had won an Olympic medal.
2. Turtle had won her first chess game from the master—Julian Eastman, alias Sam Westing.
3. Angela and Denton did finally marry each other. Eastman knew that Angela was the bomber.
4. Answers will vary.

Spotlight Literary Skill: Plot

The sentences should be numbered as follows: 6, 3, 5, 15, 11, 2, 9, 8, 10, 12, 4, 13, 14, 1, and 7.

Crossword Puzzle